Just Make Time

Jody Holland

ISBN: 0983983569
ISBN-13: 978-0-9839835-6-9

DEDICATION

This book is dedicated to all of the leaders out there who are trying to get more life out of their days. We dedicate this book to those who are striving to "Just Make Time" for the things that matter and protect their time from the things that detract from what matters.

CONTENTS

ACKNOWLEDGMENTS

I would like to acknowledge Elaine Hand for outlining the concept of "Just Make Time" and my editor, and Mom, Rita Holland for being the grammar police for me.

1 INTRODUCTION BY ELAINE HAND

"Oh great, this is just what I need… one more book on time management. I already have too much to do as it is without adding more thing to it. I have a calendar on my phone and I don't want a lesson on using it!"

If you are like me, I had said this the last several times that I was introduced to a time management concept. I didn't want to learn the seven ways to use a calendar. I just needed to know how to make time for the things that mattered most and how to avoid the rest. Out of that need, my friend and mentor, Jody Holland, and I came up with the idea of "Just Make Time." Jody has put together a fantastic representation of what it takes to keep your life in balance without giving up success in any area. He embodies the intent of the message in this book in his every day life. He just makes time for the things that truly matter the most.

What is "Just Make Time?" How is this going to help me in MY life? In 2006, I began formulating the idea of managing my life by purposely allowing only the most important things into my time. This lead to some significant changes for me and some amazing results in life. After meeting Jody, we began to hone the concept into something that could be easily taught to anyone. We didn't want a concept of managing time because time is finite. It can't be managed. It can only be filled with what matters the most. We, therefore, put together a process that is practical and easy to implement. It isn't magic.

Like most people, the concept of time management has been a pretty mysterious concept throughout my career. I would tell myself that there is never going to be enough time to get everything done. It seemed that no matter what I was doing, there was more work than day. After years of beating myself up, I seriously considered caving in and telling myself to just do the best that I could and let myself off the hook. After all, we have all been there. That wouldn't be so bad, would it? "I just don't have the time to get that done" had become a daily part of my speech. Whether it is personal, business, social, physical or spiritual, we accept that excuse. After all, it simply couldn't be our fault! Right?

When I talk with my clients about their needs to be successful – one of the main topics is always managing their time – or helping others manage theirs – or just having enough time to get everything done. It is an age old problem and it is all up to you to find the solution. Now, you ask yourself, WHAT?? That is why I am reading this book and you tell me it is all up to me. Sure it is, with an open honest look at yourself and how you do what you do when you have to, you will be able to bring clarity to your life!

There is nothing particularly new or magical in my book about Just Making Time – just clear cut guidelines and one heck of a saying to keep in your mind every time you start anything, at any given time, on any given day. It is not easy – in fact, it is very, very hard……………..yet your life, attitude and time for yourself without that dreaded worry hanging over your head will occur. It begins with you making a choice to accept responsibility to "Just Make Time."

Remember – some people do have the time to do what they want to do, when they want to do it and get it all done – you know them, right? You envy them! What do they do differently than you? How do they do it? They have the same 24 hours in the day as you. What is their secret!? One little saying to remember and ask yourself every time you start something, at any given time, on any given day is… "Will this activity get me closer to my goals in any of the five areas of the wheel of life?" If the answer is no, then you know that you need to let it go and keep focused on the things that will matter the most.

If you are ready to accept responsibility as well as accountability – just sit back, and enjoy, yes enjoy being vulnerable with yourself and your management of life. For when you manage your life, you will "Just Make Time" for what truly matters!

2 THE WHEEL OF LIFE

The wheel of life is not a brand-new concept. The idea of figuring out how to stay balanced in life has been around since the beginning of mankind. The misconception that most people make, however, is that they try to make sure that they do really well in one domain of life and lose sight of the others. When you look at each of the five key areas in the wheel of life, you begin to realize that most of us are out of balance. Addiction to work, addiction to family, addictions in your social life, even addiction to your spiritual or mental/thought life happen on a daily basis. Whenever we focus too much on one area and not enough on equalizing all areas, we find ourselves out of balance. The just make time concept says that you simply have to schedule what you want to focus on. The amount of time required for each of the five areas will be different for you than it is for me. There isn't a magic formula that says this is the exact amount of time that you have to spend with your family. There is, however, a set of signals that your brain will give off when you're not spending the right amount of time. A big part of learning to just make time is learning to set the proper goals for each one of these five areas.

Each generation tends to want to teach the next generation how to do it better than they did. You'll hear parents say things like, "Don't spend all of your time at the office!" Or, you may hear them say things like, "Make sure that you focus more on work than I did, and get a good education." The problem with advice from most people is that it is the advice that they should have taken and not the advice that you need. I want to give you a set of questions that will help you work through how much time is needed for each of the five areas in the wheel of life.

1. Fill in the following blank with one word that would describe your family. ____________

   ____

2. Fill in the blank with one word that would describe your work or your job. ________

   ____

3. Fill in the blank with one word that would

   describe your social life. _______________

   ____

4. Fill in the blank with one word that would

   describe your spiritual life. _____________

   ____

5. Fill in the blank with one word that would

   describe your mental/thought life. _______

   ____

The life that each of us lives is simply a result of the choices that we have made. You are who you are and where you are in this life because you've chosen to be in that exact spot. If you're like me, you're probably thinking the same thing that I was thinking the first time that I heard someone say something similar.

> "You're a jerk and I don't like you. I didn't choose to be in the spot that I'm in right now. It's the circumstances of life that put me here. You have no idea what I'm going through."

I wasn't very happy the first time that my business

coach told me I had chosen the situation that I was in. The truth of the matter, though, was that the choices that I had made, based on the circumstances of life, had continued pushing me in the direction that I was going. It was at the moment that I decided to take control of what I allowed in my life that my life changed. I want to share a story with you.

Jake was like most other 29-year-olds. He was a very driven individual who wanted to accomplish great things with his life. Jake was married to the woman of his dreams. In fact, they were high school sweethearts. They had been together since they were 15 years old. They got married when they were 19 years. Both of them went to college and both of them graduated from college. They had big dreams about what they were going to accomplish in life and where life was going to take them. When Jake was young, his father would continuously tell him that he was responsible for every aspect of his life. Jake didn't really like hearing that because he was often in situations that weren't that perfect. As long as he was at home, he went along with what his father said. At some point in his life, in his early 20s, and after college graduation, Jake stopped being responsible for Jake. He began to get upset with what the world was throwing at him. He worked very hard in college and he even kept a job as he went through school. He made decent grades and his teachers liked him. When he and his wife decided to have children, things began to change. Her priority shifted to wanting to raise the family and away from work. Jake was excited that she wanted to be a stay-at-home mom. He felt that it would be great for his children to have their mom, who was a wonderful person, at home with them during their formative years. It had always been easy for Jake to keep up with the family before kids came along. After all, his wife was pretty self-sufficient. At 26 years old, Jake and his wife had their first child. Jacob was a good-looking little kid, but he had a few issues. He had really bad allergies even as an infant. This kept Jacob up at night and consequently kept his parents up as well.

When Jake began getting tired, he began getting cranky. He and his wife didn't get along as well as they used to. When things would go wrong at home, Jake would divert his attention away from that area of life and towards his work. He started doing better and better at work and even received a couple of promotions. When he started doing better at work and worse at home, he also began to diverting attention away from his spiritual well-being. Once he started diverting away from his spiritual life, the friends that he and his wife had hung out with began to seem more irritating as well. He began spending even more time at work and even less time with his family, with their friends, and with his spiritual well-being. At 29 years old, Jake found himself in a situation where his wife no longer wanted to be with him. He was upset and did not want to accept responsibility for the problems that existed between the two of them. The truth of the matter in any relationship is that you do have to "just make time." His counselor had told him that.

When we begin getting out of balance in any area of life, it begins to pull us from each of the other four areas. In order for Jake to get his life back on track, he had to set solid goals and plan his time in each of the five areas. What I would like for you to do next is to write out a description of where you would like to see yourself one year from today. You will write two or three sentences about what life is actually like for you one year from today in each of the five areas on the wheel of life. So, grab your pen and focus on the future. Fill in the blanks and write out your several sentences as if it were that actual day.

Today is (one year from today) ________________. I spend __________ hours per week focusing on my family.

Today is (one year from today) ________________. I spend __________ hours per week focusing on my work.

Today is (one year from today) ________________. I spend __________ hours per week focusing on my social life.

Today is (one year from today) ________________. I spend __________ hours per week focusing on my spiritual life.

Today is (one year from today) ________________. I spend __________ hours per week focusing on my mental/thought life.

The following is a description of my family. (Keep in mind that this is a description of what is the perfect situation exactly one year from today.)

____

____

____

____

____

The following is a description of my work. (Keep in mind that this is a description of what is the perfect situation exactly one year from today.)

____

____

____

____

____

The following is a description of my social life. (Keep in mind that this is a description of what is the perfect situation exactly one year from today.)

____

____

____

____

____

The following is a description of my spiritual life. (Keep in mind that this is a description of what is the perfect situation exactly one year from today.)

____

____

____

____

____

The following is a description of my mental/thought life. (Keep in mind that this is a description of what is the perfect situation exactly one year from today.)

____

____

____

____

____

Now that we have written out what is ideal, we will need to know the steps that will get us there. There are four steps that we must follow.

1. Organize-being organized will mean something different to you than it does to me. Some people, when they are organized, have color-coded and labeled and sorted everything in their life. For others, being organized will simply mean that you know where everything is. This is not a book on how to be organized in one specific way. As a simple rule, you will

know that you are as organized as you need to be when you can find anything that you need in two minutes or less. This is what we call our two-minute rule. If you can find it in six seconds, then that is two minutes or less. If you can find it in 119 seconds, you're still good. What I do recommend that everyone does is get rid of the nonessentials in your life. Many of us are disorganized, not because we can't keep up with things, but because we have too many things to keep up with. Don't keep magazines for years that you "might go back and read an article in." Don't keep clothes that don't fit you. Don't pay for storage for stuff that you're never going to look at again. If you haven't used it in a year, it's time to get rid of it. You need to be aggressive about getting rid of the things that take away from your ability to stay on top of your life. This is a focus that you must have in order to stay on top of things and hit your targets in the wheel of life. It is now merely a recommendation, but more of a strong push in the right direction.

The second aspect of being organized, after you clear the clutter, is to **have a roadmap**. When you use the wheel of life, you are setting yourself up to understand which lanes on the highway of life will get you to your desired destination. You are creating a winning plan. By planning to win, you do. Having this roadmap, or this plan, means that you have an actual destination that you're headed towards in life. John Wooten once said, "if you fail to plan, then you are planning to fail." Taking the time to map out what your perfect destination is in each of the five areas of the wheel of life. Then, list something that you can do right now, today, in each of those areas that will move you forward.

Prioritize-we let way too many things into our life. We give time to people who give us nothing in return. We participate in activities that do not fit with our goals and objectives for life simply because we can't say no. We spin our wheels in hopes of not offending other people, hope crushing our own soul. Prioritizing is as much about what we don't let in as it is about what we do let into our life. A simple procedure that can help you map out what you will and will not let in is to identify the 3 to 5 things that are most important for your success in each of the areas of the wheel of life. If you accomplish three things per day at work, you've actually had a really good day. If you accomplish three things per day related to your family, they've had a great day. If you accomplish three things per day related to your spiritual life, you will stay more emotionally stable. If you accomplish three things per day related to your social life, you will find the joy that you've been looking for. The problem for most of us is that we don't try to accomplish three things per day in any given area. Instead, we try to accomplish 100 things in a day in only one area. In the space below, write out the three things that are most important in each of the areas of the wheel of life. These of the three things that need to happen on a daily basis. An example would be saying something nice to my family. This focuses on developing the relationships that you have with your family. An example in your social life would be to connect with a friend. Whatever the three things are that are right for you, you need to do them on a regular basis. So, fill in the blanks below and let's get started prioritizing balance in your life.

Family: ______________________________

____

____

Work: _______________________________

____

____

Social: ________________________________

____

____

Spiritual: ______________________________

____

____

Mental/Thought Life: ____________________

____

____

Evaluate - the next step in the process is to evaluate. This is one of those steps that many people will simply skip over. We work diligently to decide what we are going to put into our lives, and then very seldom do we go back and look at whether or not that's

> working. Just like you would do if you were solving a problem in business, you have to have the right steps for evaluating whether or not your priorities are getting you where you want to be. There are three questions that must be asked and answered in order to determine if you are on track. To make sure that you understand the importance of this, I want to give you a quick analogy.

Imagine that you are the starting quarterback for an NFL team. You have lead your team to the Super Bowl. The excitement is intense and you believe that your team is ready. You give them a pep talk before you head towards the corridor and then onto the field. You talk about scoring more touchdowns than the other team. You talk about stopping them from making progress. You talk about how great it's going to feel to win. Something strange happens though, when you head onto the field. There are no scoreboards at either end of the field. Slightly confused, you approach one of the referees. "Excuse me, sir. I noticed that there are no scoreboards. Can you tell me what's up with that?" "Yeah I can tell you what's going on. I will let you know whether you won or lost at the end of the game." "So, we won't know the score during the game?" "That's right kid. Now, go play the game." You play the game to the best of your ability. You started with a strategy before you left the locker room and you stayed with that strategy throughout the entire game. You go back to the locker room at halftime and assume you're doing okay. You play the second half with the same strategy that you started the first half. At the end of the game, the referee calls you and the other starting quarterback over. He tells you that the other team has won.

If you had known that you were two touchdowns behind at half-time, I would venture to guess that you would've changed your strategy. The same thing is true for the way that you handle your business. The reason that you evaluate on a regular basis is so that you know what the actual score is. If you don't know the score at half time for your life, you might continue playing with the wrong strategy. Evaluation is the key to knowing whether or not you need to change the strategy that you are using. So, let's get started on those three questions.

1. Am I feeling stress and disappointment in any of the areas on the wheel of life? If you answer yes to this question, then one of those areas is very likely out of balance. There's a good chance that you're spending too much time on another area and not enough time on this area.
2. Am I getting the results that I intended to get in each of the areas of the wheel of life? If you find that you are not getting the results that you are looking for, you may have the wrong strategy or the wrong focus. Strategy is your tactical implementation as you pursue your goals. Focus is where your attention goes during the tactical implementation. If you find that your mind seems to wander during the

implementation, it is likely a focus issue.

3. Do I feel fulfilled by putting my time and energy into the things that I've chosen to invest them in? If you are lacking fulfillment, then you need to reassess what you are just making time for. If you are fulfilled, then chances are high that you are on track.

The last component of checking for balance is being honest with yourself and with others. The hardest word in the English language is not "sorry." The hardest word in the English language is "no." One of the keys to being able to just make time for the things that are truly important is being able to eliminate the things that are taking up your time that are unimportant. We spend so much of our time trying not to offend people or hurt their feelings. The reality is that we do not pour our heart and our soul into the things that don't really matter to us. You're much better off to simply let people know that you can't make time for that. Never forget that you only have a finite, or limited, amount of time. You can't create more or buy more or manifest more time. You can only choose what you just make time for and what you don't make time for. The key is to choose as wisely as possible. I have an assignment for you here. Within the next 48 hours, I want you to tell someone "no" that asks you to invest time in something that is not that important to you. Don't try to evaluate whether or not it's important overall. Simply evaluate whether or not it is important to you and whether it fits with where you are going. We have both had to learn the hard lesson of telling great volunteer organizations that we would not be on their board or volunteer with them. We have both chosen the organizations that mean the most to us where we will be passionate about investing our time.

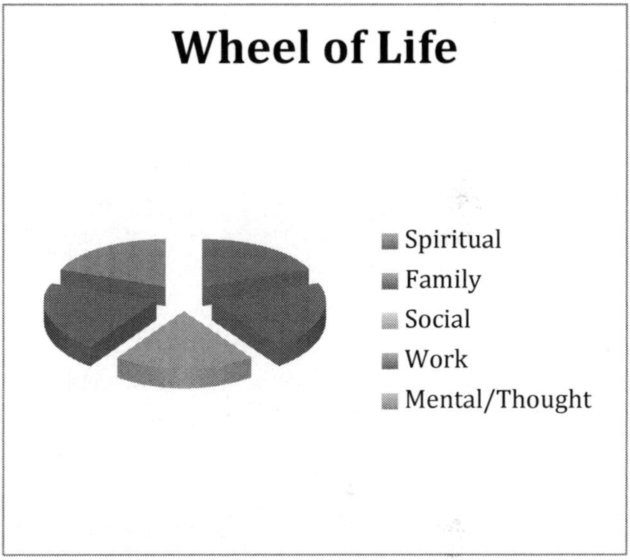

3 DOING WHAT YOU HAVE TO DO

Sometimes a leader has to do what a leader has to do. A big part of my job as a leader is to make sure that I do the right things for the right reasons. It is no different for you than it is for me. In the words of Stephen Covey in his book First Things First, "the main thing is to keep the main thing the main thing." I would argue that you would be significantly more effective in your life if you understood at a very clear level how to be in balance. The reason that you make time for the things that are most important is because it allows you to fulfill your true purpose in this world. When you don't make time for the things that are most important, you find yourself running around like crazy simply trying to keep up. The following is a list of things that I believe are justification for doing what you have to do when you have to do it. Take a look at them and then add others that you feel drive you.

Why develop your Just Make Time skills…

- Bringing balance to your life: each of us finds the greatest level of satisfaction and fulfillment in life when we are in balance. Understanding how to balance between the wheel of life, like you learned in Chapter 2, positions you for living a happy and fulfilled life.
- Reducing stress: a moderate amount of the right kind of stress can be extremely motivating. Having said that, I have only met a few people that had a moderate amount of the right kind of stress in their life. Most people have excessive amounts of the wrong kind of stress. The wrong kind of stress causes all kinds of physical problems. We manifest problems in our health when we allow stress to build up and begin tearing us down.
- Planning and organizing: planning exactly what you will make time for sets you apart from the rest of the crowd. People who have a plan for the daily behaviors and activities that they will engage tend to organize their thoughts and their actions more effectively. When you organize on purpose, you don't allow roadblocks into your plan.
- Taking better care of yourself: every year, in January, I see several hundred extra people at the gym. I reference only the month of January because they're not there in February. When you make time for exercise and for eating right, you make a lifestyle choice.

Unless you schedule time to take care of yourself, you will end up like most Americans who simply don't take care of themselves.

- Improving communication: communicating effectively is a very intentional act. If we do not intentionally communicate who we are and what our expectations are for what is allowed in our time, we will tend to get drug down by our circumstances. People who have a plan for what they will make time for are the same people who are very clear about what they intend for their life. For example, if you are asked to volunteer for something and you had already planned that timeslot for something else, you wouldn't tell the person maybe. You would let them know that you are already booked for something else so that they could go find another volunteer. This deliberate act eliminates the organization from calling you back repeatedly and using up your time and theirs to try to convince you to make a decision. Just say no and allow them to move on.
- Seizing new opportunities: people who take action on a daily basis towards their specific goals and objectives seem to have the universe coordinate opportunities for them. When you are living with a definite purpose, other people take notice. When they take notice, they attempt to coordinate opportunities for you. It may seem that the universe is conspiring for your success. The truth of the matter is that you simply planned to be successful and eliminated the things that kept

you from being successful.

- Personal development: developing your self into the best version of you is something that takes time. In Tony Robbins' program, "Get The Edge," he refers to this personal development time as your "hour of power." It is amazing to me the number of people who simply choose not to read books once they are done with their formal education. If you do not allot time for developing "you," this will very often take a back burner to things that seem more urgent. Never allow the tyranny of the urgent to destroy the importance of your priorities.
- Professional development: according to John Maxwell, in The 21 Irrefutable Laws of Leadership, each of us has a lid on our professional capabilities. We are not able to develop the people below us to any higher than one step below where we are. This means that if we want to develop our teams, we must first develop ourselves. Becoming the best professional "you" possible means that you truly care about the success of the people that work for you. It means that you want to offer them more than you were able to offer them before. A personal challenge that each of us was given was to read one professional development book per month for the rest of our lives. People who read one professional development book per month are listed in the top 1% intellectually in this country. I don't know about you, but that's the exact place I want to be listed.

What you decide to do with your life is ultimately up to you. As a leader in your respective field, knowing what to limit and knowing what to include are two critical factors for your success. The idea organizing and managing is not something that is extremely fun to me. However, I see the incredible value in staying on top of the things that go into my day. I've built up enough positives about being organized and enough negatives about not keeping track of my day that it made perfect sense to take action. It is not your circumstances that control what you get done during the day. There are things that distract you from your objective. I'm not saying that every day will be perfect after reading this book. What I am saying is that you have to make a choice. The theme of this entire book is to choose to just make time. The choice that you make is your choice. What I would like for you to do is to write a list of the positives of controlling what goes into your time and a list of the negatives of not controlling what goes into your time.

4 A CHANGING WORLD

The world we live in today is not the same as the world that we used to live in. When I think back to my own childhood, I remember what it was like to sit and watch the news with my father. When Walter Cronkite was on the news, it was just Walter. There was nothing else on the screen. He would come on and let us know what was going on and then he would go off. Nothing scrolled across the screen. There were no pictures inside the pictures. There was no upcoming story. There was just Walter. I believe that we're trying to cram more into our time than we have ever tried to cram before. I don't think that this is making us a happier society. I think the simple reality is we are trying to make time fit into our schedules instead of making our schedules fit into time. We haven't learned how to say no or how to limit ourselves.

In a study conducted by Pitney Bowes Inc. and San Jose State University, in late 1996, they looked at 1000 companies and what interrupted them, or kept them from accomplishing what they needed to on a daily basis. They received responses from 972 employees from those Fortune 1000 companies. It revealed that, in 1996, the average executive received 178 messages each day. These were in a combination of telephone calls, emails, voicemails, and other mediums. 84% of respondents indicated that at least three times per hour they were interrupted by messages. And don't forget, this was in 1996! In my informal surveys with a few hundred companies that I work with, the average executive is interrupted significantly more than 178 times a day. We get a lot more emails than we used to get. We get Facebook notifications now as well. There are so many ways to get in touch with us electronically that there isn't a "shut off" button for our socially intertwined lives. The simple reality for executives today is they have to take control of their time. They have to just make time for the things that actually matter. And they have to protect their time from the things that don't matter. According to the financial express article in January 2006, interruptions consume 2.1 hours a day or 28% of the average workday. Most executives were not fully focused again until 25 minutes after the interruption. This means it that we're going through our day not fully focused.

One of the fundamental points that we intend for you to get through this book is that you have to make time for what matters. You can't allow the world to control your time. You have a very limited supply. The following are five hints that will help you in this changing world to control your time.

1. Give yourself a timeout. Take a specified amount of time, say 30 minutes, at either the end or the very beginning of each day. This is your planning time. You should not have your email open. You should not be taking phone calls. You should not allow people to walk into your office during this time. This is your time to reflect on the previous day's work and to plan for tomorrow's work. Many people go through their day trying to scramble and figure out what is important. By taking time out to plan, you've already established your path and your priorities. Giving yourself this time to plan prevents you from having to work as much overtime. It prevents you from allowing things into your life that really don't matter. It keeps you on track and keeps you sane.
2. Be the boss of your technology. Technology can be an absolutely wonderful thing, if it's used in the right way. Set up auto responders on your email to let people know when you're not available. Schedule for your emails to go out at a very specific time in order to control when people see information. Hit the “do not disturb” button on your cell phone at a certain time in the evening. When you start working in blocks of 15 to 30 minutes at a time, you will get more and more comfortable with keeping technology out of your way while you

work. One example would be that it is ideal to go through and mark specific emails as spam that are irrelevant to you. By limiting the number of emails that come to your actual inbox, you prepare yourself for being truly successful. Most executives will receive over 200 emails in an average day. More than 80% of all emails that are sent in the United States on a daily basis are actually spam. This means, there might be 40 realistic emails to look at for the average executive. Learning how to work your technology and setting up your technology to work for you makes your life much easier. Utilize technology in your hiring processes to make things work smoother and more quickly. Utilize technology, such as GoTo Meeting ® in meetings so that you don't have to travel as much. Sometimes it is a good idea to stand face-to-face with a client or prospect. However, many times, they are just as busy as you are and would appreciate a shorter meeting that gets to the point.

3. Strategically design your meetings to meet your needs. In any meeting that you attend, make sure that there is a point. Do not attend meetings for the sake of attending meetings. It is an excellent idea to have a standup or quick information meeting first thing in the morning with your staff. By doing this, each person receives between 45 and 60 seconds to indicate what they have on tap for the day. This lets everyone know the direction of each of the key players. During your weekly meetings, this is designed to give you an

overview of what was accomplished in the past week and what is coming up for the next week. It is not intended to be a strategy session. Your monthly meetings overview short-term strategy and adjust priorities in order to stay on track with your quarterly and annual goals. These meetings should not be more than two hours in length. Quarterly planning meetings can be up to three hours long. These dig into the short-term and long-term strategies that you are using to meet your goals. It is important to map out specific tactics to go with your strategies during these meetings. Once per year, is ideal to go away with your staff for one to two days as an executive. You should do your annual planning and celebrate your successes for the year. By keeping your meetings organized and relevant, you will actually limit the number of meetings that you conduct. The ones that you do conduct, will provide value to you and to the members of your team.

4. Create some boundaries. When each of us went into business in the very beginning, we wanted to be on every nonprofit board that asked. We both love to help people, and really enjoyed being needed as well. We found ourselves on upwards of seven boards each. That will produce between seven and 21 meetings per month to participate in. While it can be difficult to know which nonprofit gets the axe, we highly recommend that you pick only two. Choose the nonprofits that mean the most to you. These should be the ones

that you would be passionate about no matter what. Everyone has a cause, but you need to identify which cause most closely resembles your belief system. You have to train yourself to say no to great opportunities to volunteer. Only say yes to two at a time. If a third board comes along and you think that it is the best board that you have ever seen in your entire existence, then decide which of the other two has to go. Keep in mind, your objective should be to stay balanced with the wheel of life. When you volunteer too much, it takes away from your family and from your job. When you volunteer too little, you don't receive the fulfillment that you need in your life. Two is my number. Your number may be different. Whatever your number is, make a decision about it and stick to it.

5 I'M NOT AVERAGE

If you're an average American, each week you watch television for 25 hours, read for just under three hours, and receive the majority of your phone calls between 10 and 11 AM. I hear people asking questions like, where do you find time to write a book. The first thing that I would say, is we shouldn't try to be an average American. For that matter, you shouldn't try to be average at anything. I'm always striving to be better than average. That means, perhaps I spend less than 25 hours in an average week watching television. I utilize my commute time from the office to home and back in order to listen the audiobooks. I'm able to get in more than three hours of listening to audiobooks on a weekly basis. Our lives are full of things that don't necessarily get us closer to where we want to be. As you evaluate the things that are in your life, look for the things that you can limit. For example, what if you limited your television watching to no more than one hour per day? That would mean, that you just found 18 hours that you could do something else every week. That's like a good part-time job.

According to the Bureau of Labor Statistics, and their American Time Use Survey, we spend over 70% of our adult lives working and/or doing work related things. These things could include commuting, thinking or talking about projects, planning out what we need to accomplish the next day, or even stressing about what we did not get done. While I do find work very fulfilling and very important, I doubt that I will say on my deathbed, "I wish that I had spent more time in the office." I really don't know of anyone that would make that statement at the end of their life. I have found that having my quiet time, that 30 minutes per day that I talked about in the last chapter, helps me not to think about work when I'm at home. Zig Ziglar used to say in his speeches, “It's no wonder that people are so worn out. While you're at work, your mind is on things from your home. While you're at home, your mind is on things at work. Your mind is always racing to somewhere else and your body can't keep up." This can lead to what is known as social jet lag. Average people suffer from this. Let's explore exactly what it is.

Each of us has a circadian rhythm to our body. These are the internal biological clocks that regulate many of the functions and activities that we participate in. They include things like sleep, temperature of the body, your metabolism, alertness and attentiveness, blood pressure, heart rate, hormone levels, and even your immunities. Your body cycles through these rhythms of metabolic and chemical changes every 24 hours. Your circadian rhythms are reset by sunlight each morning. Whether or not you are a morning person or a night owl is determined by your circadian rhythm. These circadian rhythms have a tremendous impact on our society. There are two peak times during a 24-hour period when a person would be susceptible to falling asleep. These times are between 3 AM and 5 AM, and in between 3 PM and 5 PM. Have you ever noticed that around 3 o'clock in the afternoon you start thinking about needing more coffee or an energy drink? It isn't necessarily the fact that you had a good meal for lunch. It's the rhythm of your body. People naturally synchronize their internal clocks with daytime and nighttime cycles. This allows them to be awake during the day and sleep during the night, which is how we were biologically designed. Your body regulates your circadian rhythms primarily through your eyes. Light stimulates nerves in the retina that pass signals through a chain of nerves to the brain. When, for example, bright light stimulates the optic nerves, the optic nerves then send a signal to the brain, which then triggers circadian rhythms, resulting in the synchronization of the body's 24 hour cycle with the Earth's rhythm. That would mean, that staring at a bright screen one hour before bedtime, will generally result in stimulating your circadian rhythm and making it more difficult for you to fall asleep. The average person now keeps their cell phone beside their bed. Many people read on their iPad, or other electronic readers. When a person does this, they set themselves up for not sleeping as well. Other people watch television right before they go to bed, or try to sleep with the TV on. This also stimulates the circadian rhythm and makes it more difficult to rest the way the body was intended. So, it can really pay to not be an average person. Restrict yourself from looking at your phone, E reader, or your TV set within an hour of when you intend to go to sleep. This will help your body get in rhythm and prepare for rest.

When we learn to listen to our bodies, it becomes much easier to work with these natural rhythms, instead of fighting against them. It is ideal that you schedule out your activities based on when your rhythms are in sync. Your time, and your life, become much more efficient when you do certain activities at certain times of the day. Anyone who has traveled has experienced jet lag at some point. Jet lag is that groggy realization that while your day is beginning in Massachusetts, your night is hardly over in California. If you are a morning person, someone who gets up several hours before the normal person does, what I'm about to tell you will need to be shifted backwards a couple of hours. If you are a night owl, someone who barely goes to bed before the sun comes up, you'll need to shift these activities forward a couple of hours.

Cognitive tasks are generally performed best between 8 AM and noon. These are tasks such as reading, performing calculations, solving problems, or writing. If you are cramming for a test, or doing any kind of a last minute review for presentation, this is performed best between 6 AM and 10 AM. Staying up into the middle of the night to study for a test is generally ineffective. You do better to get up early in prep for the test. And you do even better to have studied for this test a long time ago. Remember to plan what you put into each day so that when it becomes crunch time, your life doesn't really change. You are already prepared! If you are sleep deprived, you are destroying your capacity for short term memory. You're also hindering your ability for long-term memory skills. Longer-term memory tasks, such as memorizing speeches or information for an application are best performed in the afternoon. Your mental abilities and your physical functions coordinate with your body temperature. Between 1 PM and 4 PM, you are at the ideal bodily temperature for long-term memory. Your capacity for manual dexterity peaks between 2 PM and 6 PM. This is the best time for you to perform tasks such as typing, carpentry work, or just about anything that requires the use of your hands. I know that lots of trainers will tell you that you should work out very first thing in the morning to kick start your metabolism, which are more likely to injure yourself then. Your large muscle coordination is at its peak between 4 PM and 9 PM. This means, you will perceive the work out to be easier when you work out in the evening, rather than in the morning. You can even improve your sleep quality if you work out five hours before you intend to go to bed. It's not a good idea to work out right before you intend to go to bed, though.

When you are out of rhythm with what the body was intended to do, that's when you suffer from social jet lag. Here are a few questions that you can answer there will let you know whether your suffering, or likely to suffer from social jet lag.

1. Do you get up about the same time morning?
2. Do you wake up without an alarm most mornings?
3. Do you almost always get between seven and nine hours of sleep per night?

If you answered no to any of these questions, it's likely that you suffer from social jet lag at least a little bit. This is particularly true when your sleep patterns are abnormal or are disturbed on a regular basis. That's why you see so many new parents walking around looking out of rhythm. The symptoms of jet lag are not that pleasant. They include things like…

- constipation
- clammy sweat
- diarrhea
- earache
- fatigue
- headaches
- hemorrhoids
- impaired coordination
- impaired vision
- anxiety
- impatience
- insecurity
- insomnia
- irregular heartbeat
- lightheadedness
- loss of libido

- low blood sugar
- memory loss
- nausea
- susceptibility to illness
- and generally being in a bad mood

Not keeping our bodies in rhythm will affect us physically, mentally, and emotionally. One of the best thing that you can do is…

JUST MAKE TIME FOR WHAT MATTERS

Stress causes our internal rhythms to lose that synchronicity. It overrides our natural circadian rhythm, which affects sleep, eating, and all other bodily functions. This stress response is the same as if you were physically wounded or losing blood. Your immune system begins to break down, which leads to weakness and susceptibility to illnesses. It also makes it much easier to injure yourself and much harder to heal yourself.

Physical stressors can include things such as temperature, sound, vibration, movement, and even too much humidity. Physiological stressors include sleep disturbance, not eating regularly, overconsumption of alcohol, the use of nicotine, and even the use of caffeine.

When you don't get enough sleep, you dull your sensory perceptions, such as vision and hearing. You lengthen your reaction time, slow down your motor coordination, reduce memory retrieval, lower new memorization ability, and generally become irritable to be around. Plan on keeping yourself in rhythm, getting enough sleep, and making time for what matters the most. When you do this, you end up not being just the average person. You end up being the kind of person who can easily make time for what matters most. I want you to be in rhythm and I want you to be extraordinary!

6 DON'T PROCRASTINATE – THE PAIN AND PLEASURE PRINCIPLE

Why put off till tomorrow what you can do today? That is a good question indeed. It seems that there aren't really a lot of good answers to this question, though. Most people can't verbalize why they have not done what they know is necessary for success. They understand, at a logical level, what the required behaviors or activities are, but they can't seem to make themselves move forward. This has its significant costs to the person and their pocketbook.

Procrastination has shifted the tide of wealth, and not in a good way. It seems that the richest place on earth isn't a country or even a region, though. The richest place on earth is the graveyard. This is the place where all of the unwritten books, the unlived dreams, the un-started entrepreneurial ventures, and the unfulfilled promises reside. There are more unfulfilled riches in the graveyard than anywhere else on earth. The big question, though, is why?

William James, the Father of American psychology, said that there are only two motivators in the human psyche. Those two motivators are the avoidance of pain and the pursuit of pleasure. When you think about it, everything that we do in life could be explained in one of those two directions. We were avoiding actual, or more often, imagined pain when we did not take the actions that could have moved us forward in life. It is only when the real or perceived pleasure of an activity is great enough that we take action. Most people want to complicate things more than this, but it really is that simple. We avoid pain, real or perceived. We pursue pleasure, real or perceived.

Procrastination could be defined as choosing to avoid a task or decision with the understanding that doing so will make things worse for you, but not right now. This "pain delay" principle is used regularly by people all around this globe. The part of this definition that is the most fascinating, though, is that people know that they will be worse off. They know that taking action now would actually make it better. If you have ever told someone that you work better under pressure, then you have intentionally made things worse for yourself. Taking specific "non-action" in order to find a way to actually motivate yourself towards action later generally leads to a worse product or service. This means that procrastination could really be traced back to a matter of motivation. If you can identify the best ways to motivate yourself toward action now, then you will be able to avoid the pain of procrastination and attain the pleasure of less stress while you achieve success.

Think about someone who is wanting to start an exercise program and lose some weight. They wake up at 5 AM, groggy and tired, and think… "maybe tomorrow." The pain of getting out of bed and foregoing an hour or more of sleep can seem too great. The pain of getting out of bed is greater than the pleasure of being in shape and healthy. Suppose your physician tells you that you have to exercise or you won't make it another year. All of a sudden, getting up at 5AM and going to the gym makes perfect sense and you take action. The motivation for them was the idea that they no longer had a choice about the exercise. They had to take action now. This isn't any different than a person who "works best under pressure." In order to begin creating the motivation that you need to achieve the results that you really want, you have to have the right levels of energy.

Building up your positive energy and tearing down the negative takes a specific focus. Think about something in your life that you have really wanted to achieve. When you thought about that end result, you likely experienced a sense of joy and accomplishment, or a sense of relief. It is the emotion that drives the motion. Your job is to fulfill the laws of physics in your daily activity.

A body in motion tends to stay in motion. A body at rest tends to stay at rest.

This isn't just relative to understanding the velocity of an object. It is relative to understanding the velocity of your success. You have to be that "body in motion." In order to achieve that, you begin to build up positive energy about the things that you need to do and begin to build up negative energy about not doing the things that you need to do. Let's say, for example, that you want to start making more sales calls. You will need to define what more means and then you will need to find a way to "feel" like doing it. Let's say that you want to make 15 sales calls per week, or 3 per day, 5 days per week. In order to connect with 3 people, you will likely have to make 9 calls. In order to do that, you will need about 1 hour, maybe up to 2 hours. As an exercise, please fill in the blanks below about the 10 benefits that you could achieve by increasing the number of sales calls that you make in a week. Even if you are not in sales, play along here. Imagine that you are a sales person and that your purpose is to drive new business. What would be the benefits of making these connected calls every day? If you prefer to stick with what you do, then change the sales calls to any activity that is required of you to be truly successful in your job or business. The main point of the exercise is to see what the pain and pleasure principle does and how to use it for your good.

Benefits of making 3 connected sales calls per day:

1. ______________________________
2. ______________________________
3. ______________________________
4. ______________________________
5. ______________________________
6. ______________________________
7. ______________________________
8. ______________________________
9. ______________________________
10. ______________________________

How does it feel to think about all of those benefits?

Now, to make sure that this works, you will need to define the pain, or drawbacks, of not making the 3 connected calls per day. It is important that you write out all of the bad that could or would happen if you don't follow through.

1. ______________________________

2. ______________________________

3. ______________________________

4. ______________________________

5. ______________________________

6. ______________________________

7. ______________________________

8. ______________________________

9. ______________________________

10. ______________________________

How does it feel to think about all of those negatives of not taking action?

This is what I refer to as an "action-stack." It is a way of stacking your emotions in your favor in order to induce action now. You need to have enough positive emotion for the desired activity and enough negative activity against not taking action. NOW is the time to act!

When would now be a good time? Too many people in this world walk around wondering when a good time would be to take action. They wonder when "the right time" would be for them to become an entrepreneur, start painting, write a book, choose to succeed at work, or any number of other things. The truth of the matter is that "NOW" is the right time to take action and make your life what you want it to be. Now is the time that exists. There really is no future or past. There is only now. The present is the one true reality. So, the question that you have to answer for yourself is…

When would NOW be a good time to take action?

7 PARETO'S PRINCIPLE

Vilfredo Pareto was an economist, engineer, and philosopher who came up with the 80/20 rule. We have seen this rule applied over and over again in business and with respect to a variety of focus areas. Often times, it has been used in human resources to describe the concept that 20% of a company's employees produce 80% of the results. The original theory, however, had to do with land ownership in Italy. As Pareto looked at the normal distribution of land ownership, he found that 20% of people owned 80% of the land. He dug further into this premise and began discovering some very interesting correlations with his 80/20 Rule.

He found that this rule could be applied to almost anything that we do in life. It could be applied to workers. It could be applied to relationships. And, perhaps most importantly in this case, it could be applied to where we get our results. From an economic success perspective, Pareto discovered that the vast majority of success in the endeavors that we undertake could be traced back to a small amount of actions taken. It is consistently 20% of our activities that produce 80% of our results. His economic and success theory held that we needed to identify the 20% of things that would get us the greatest results and then make those things primary in our day. After all, if you don't get those things done, it would have a tremendous economic impact on you and your business. Conversely, if you didn't get something done from the 80% category, which only produced 20% of the results, it wouldn't really matter that much.

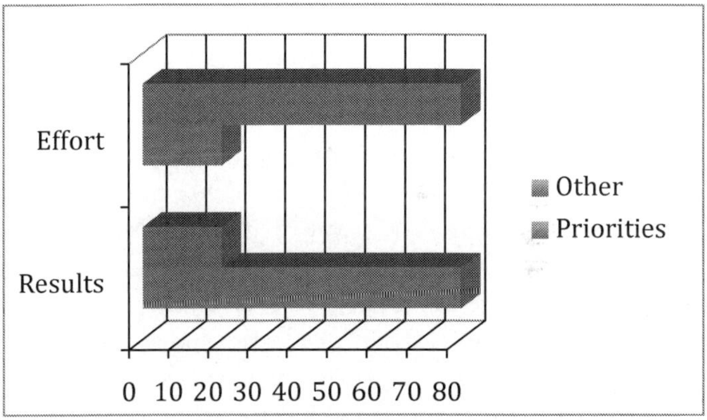

This is great news for us! This means that we simply have to figure out what matters the most and do that first. In a program that we have conducted for entrepreneurs for the last couple of decades, we have helped them discover what that 20% really is. We have seen that most people spin their wheels, so to speak, throughout the day. They do the things that are easy before the things that are hard. They do the things that they like before the ones that they dislike. They do what they know before what is unfamiliar. By taking the easy road, they miss out on the road that leads to success. The objective of this book is to help you find the road to success and prosperity, however you define that in your own life. This means that you have to first answer these two questions…

Am I willing to do what works instead of just what is easy or familiar?

☐ Yes ☐ No

If I were choosing, I would rather be:

☐ Right ☐ Successful

How you answered those two questions is very important to your success in life. If you checked "yes" on the first question and you really meant it, then you have demonstrated that you are ready to do what is necessary, even if it means that you have to stretch yourself a bit. If you answered "successful" on the second question, then you have stepped into a realm that is occupied by most of the successful people of this world. The truth is that we spend an inordinate amount of time trying to be right instead of trying to be successful.

One of the keys to learning, growing, and winning is the willingness to "unlearn" what you already know. We must be willing to unlearn, or empty our preconceived notions in order to fill our minds with new information and set up new habits for success. The next exercise for you is to determine what your 20% is. You are identifying the four most important things that you would need to do in a day in order to be successful. Keep in mind that you can only have four on the left. For the "Type A" personalities out there who believe that they have 100 critical daily tasks, this can be a daunting exercise. For those who are more balanced and big picture in their thinking, this can be freeing. Whichever type you are, the activity will be rewarding. As you think about those four things, imagine what four things you would do to be successful if you could ONLY do four things. Those are generally the ones that end up being the right answer for you. The worksheet is on the next page. Good luck and happy focusing!

On the left hand side of the worksheet, you can have no more than 4 items.

Most Important	Everything Else
1	1
2	2
3	3
4	4
	5
	6
	7
	8
	9
	10
	11
	12
	13
	14
	15
	16

This chart is designed to help you discover the 4 things that you need to do on a daily basis in order to find success. These are the four things that you MUST make time for each and every day. If you don't make time for them, you will find that you end your day with frustration and exhaustion. This stress and exhaustion happens when the 80% that produces the least results is our focus instead of the 20% that creates the greatest results. We gain energy when we know that we have done the 20% every day. We gain momentum when we focus on the things that matter the most for our success.

If you didn't fill out the chart, go back and do that now. This is one of the most important things that you can do. Pareto knew what he was talking about. He understood that it wasn't and still isn't "Just Do More" that should be your mantra. It was and still is "Just Make Time" that leads you down the path to success. The key to success in using this table is starting on the left. You should not do anything on the right hand side of the table until you have done everything on the left hand side of the table. By starting with what is important, you find that you have plenty of time for what matters most. You also figure out very quickly that most of what is on the right hand side of the table doesn't actually get you where you want to go in life.

Start On The Left And It Will Be Alright!

8 BIG ROCKS

From the book, First Things First (MERRILL, 1996), Covey, Merrill, and Merrill outline a story that they had seen unfold in a college classroom. The professor had wanted to teach his students about the importance of managing what they put into their time and had not been able to get the message across with mere lecturing. He decided to perform a demonstration that would make things more clear. We have used this same demonstration with our "Just Make Time" classes over the years as well. It is a very effective way to see the importance of putting the important things into our lives in the right order. So, as you read this, imagine that you are in front of us and you are witnessing this demonstration. Focus on getting a mental image of what this would look like as we tell it in the first person. Imagine that I am a professor and you are a student in a class that I am teaching. When you place yourself in that setting, the story has the greatest impact.

> *I want to thank you for coming to class today. Today, we have a very important lesson. I want you to pay close attention and I would really appreciate your participation. Today, we are going to talk about how to get more done in life.*

At this point, I would reach under a table and pull out a large glass jar. The jar is completely empty. I would also pull out a bowl full of large rocks, a bowl full of gravel, a bowl full of sand, and a glass of water.

> *The jar that I have here represents your life. Imagine that each of us has the same amount of space in our lives that we can fill up. We each have 24 hours in a day. We can't get more even if we really want it.*

At this point, I begin placing one large rock at a time into the jar. I continue this process until there appears to be no more space in the jar and it is full.

> *Is the jar full?*

You look at the jar and see that there isn't any way to fit another large rock into the jar. Many students will respond that the jar is indeed full at this point. If that is the case, our response is…

> *No, the jar isn't full. I am now going to add gravel into the jar. I will pour a little in and then shake the jar to make sure that it settles and then I will pour some more. Can you see how the gravel is filling the spaces of time that were left around the big rocks?*

I continue this process of pouring and shaking until the jar appears to be full. The gravel has settled all around the big rocks that were in the jar. I then ask the question of you again.

Is the jar full now?

You, like most of our students, have caught on by this point and realize that the gravel did not completely fill all spaces in the jar and you respond that the jar is not full.

I then grab the bowl with sand in it and begin to sift the sand into the jar and shake the jar, just like I did with the gravel. The sand filters through the gravel and makes its way methodically to the bottom of the jar. Pretty soon, I have added in all of the sand that I can fit. I then lift my head to look at you and I ask… Is the jar full?

You look at the jar and then let your eyes dart to the water that is sitting on the table. You get a slight smirk on your face and you respond that the jar is still not completely full.

Very good! I am going to fill the rest of the spaces in the jar with water now. I begin to pour the water in slowly and it trickles into all of the spaces in between the sand, gravel, and big rocks. It doesn't take me long to fill the jar all the way to the top. I look at you and I ask… Is the jar full?

You realize that, this time, the jar really is full. You sit back in your chair and think about how much more fit into the jar after the big rocks were placed in there.

I ask you… What is the lesson here?

You look at me and you respond confidently that one can always fit more into their life if they just try.

Now it is my turn to say… NO! The lesson here is that you will never fit the big rocks, the important things, into your life if you don't put them in first.

The reality of the world that we live in is that we are constantly being pulled in one direction or another. We often forget what the big rocks are, or should be, in our lives In the last chapter, we discussed the important things for your day. In the beginning of this book, we discussed the wheel of life. And, throughout this book, I have been talking with you about how to prioritize what you put into your time. Every time I think about the water, the sand, the gravel, and the big rocks, I think about how many things are competing for my attention. I realize that it is up to me to ensure that the right things receive it and the wrong things do not. If you have not identified what those right things are, though, you will find yourself frustrated regularly at the end of the day, wondering if it is all worth the effort.

What are the big rocks that should be in your life? A few examples of big rocks are things like…

1. Eating dinner at home a few nights a week
2. Going on dates with your spouse
3. Exercising regularly
4. Taking at least one vacation per year

5. Taking time each day to read and learn
6. Ensuring that you take time to invest in your retirement and to learn about doing this properly
7. Investing in your spiritual life
8. Going to your kid's game, or play, or other event
9. Scheduling time to write a book
10. Working with an executive or life coach

The list could go on and on. Most people don't even know what is actually important to them in life. They have not reviewed the wheel of life and discovered what really will have a lasting impact on the way in which they see the world. They have let lots of water, sand, and gravel rule their time and their life instead of living life according to their chosen "big rocks." I am glad that you won't be one of those people from this point forward. I am thankful that you believe in managing what goes into your time and making sure that you put the things that matter most into your life first. I am very glad that you will "Just Make Time" for the life that you truly desire!

Do what matters most first and success will pursue you!

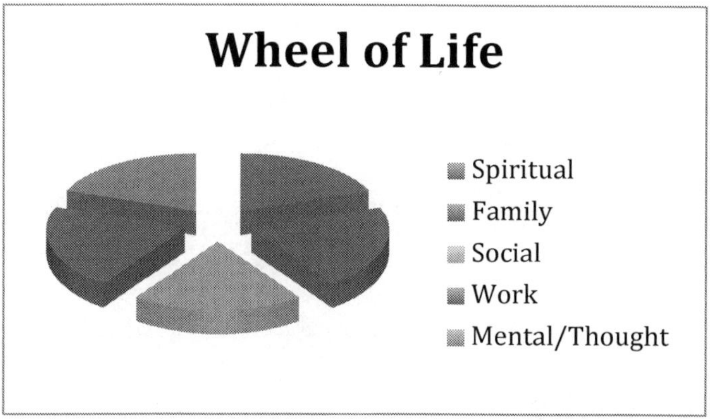

When you look at each of the areas in the wheel of life, what are the big rocks that deserve your time in each area? Do you have a balanced focus on big rocks? What will you "Just Make Time" for in this life?

A big rock in the area of my spiritual life is: ______

____

____

A big rock in the area of my family life is: _______

____

____

A big rock in the area of my social life is: ________

____

____

A big rock in the area of my work life is: ________

____

____

A big rock in the area of my mental/thought life is:

____

____

____

9 THE ONE THING

Throughout this book, you have learned that it isn't time that you are managing. It isn't your calendar that is critical. It isn't even what you accomplish that matters most. What truly matters most is who you become by understanding how to "Just Make Time" for what is most critical. As you go through your life, you will be given glorious opportunities. Some are in the right direction, while others will steer you away from your purpose. The people who go the furthest in life are those who know how to say no to the distractions and yes to the priorities.

Think about someone that you would consider to be a great leader, a true success. If you were to examine their life, you would see that it was full of struggles, challenges, and obstacles. Those are a part of every great story. I hear people complain about the struggles in life regularly. The difference between the people who focus on the problem and the people who focus on the goal is that the goal seekers never believe that anything can stop them from achieving what they desire in life. The complainers seem to only be able to see the things that can keep them from their goal. What you focus on is what you get.

Quite literally, your subconscious mind has the ability to process more than 2 million bits of information per second. Your conscious mind only has the ability to sort and organize about 1,000 bits of information per second. That means that there is a lot going on that gets categorized, distorted, and deleted. The job of the conscious mind is filter the world to ensure that only the necessary information gets dealt with. At the base of your brain is the Reticular Activating System. This is the "point of filtration." Whatever you consciously decide to focus on is what comes into attention. For example, if you were to decide to think about Ford Raptor ® pickups, you would begin to notice more of those pickups. If you were to think about things getting in your way and things going wrong, you guessed it, things will start to go wrong. You have to be very deliberate about focusing on the things that matter most. This is why the "Just Make Time" model has been so effective in my own life. I would encourage you to not take my word for it though. I want you to try it for yourself and make your own judgments about whether "Just Making Time" for the things that are important and keeping your focus on what matters is really the right plan.

A Little Proof

Every year in the United States, more than 200 million people will set goals for what they want to accomplish in January for the upcoming year. Many of those goals include things like losing weight, eating healthier, exercising more, spending time with family, and so on. These are the big rocks that they want in their life, but have not taken action on in the past. Every year in February, roughly half of the people that made goals will give up on them for the year. In fact, by June of each year, roughly 97% of all goal setters have given up on their annual dreams. The main issue is that most people don't really plan to accomplish what they say in January of the year. They are making "hope-olutions" instead of resolutions. Only about 3% of Americans set actual goals for themselves. Of those that set actual goals, including writing them out, over 97% of the goals are met. That same group of people will make, on average, 300% more money than those who don't set goals. To me, that was proof enough to start setting goals every January, including what I was going to do to attain those goals.

As if the idea of have three times the earning potential wasn't good enough, there was one more step that I learned about. People who read their goals every day, keeping them front and center, earn 20 times that of people who don't set goals. This is actually not that hard. The easiest way to accomplish this is to use what you learned in Chapter 2 of this book. The chapter on "The Wheel of Life" has you use one word to describe each of the 5 areas in your own life. Using that model, simply choose one word that describes the ideal scenario for each of the 5 areas of the Wheel of Life. For example, when you think of your mental/thought life, the word might be something like "sharp." This one word concept will help to keep you to stay focused on what you should really make time for in your daily life. It is much easier than trying to read out three goals per section or learn a business mantra or rewrite your goals on a daily basis.

My recommendation would be that you keep your one word focus areas for each of the 5 areas of the Wheel of Life on a notecard. You can print them small enough to laminate them and keep them in your wallet or purse. Every morning, very first thing, look at that card and read out loud the one word that is your model for each of the five areas. At lunch, read it out loud again. Before you go to bed, and I mean right before you go to bed, read it out loud again. By reading this out loud three times per day, your shifting your conscious focus to those areas. This means that your subconscious mind, that supercomputer that you possess, will begin to bring opportunities into your awareness that will make a big difference for you and your personal success.

I have tried experiments with this in my own life and in the lives of a thousand or so executives. With one simple process, I wanted to see how the lives and businesses of people could change. Just changing one thing, the focus area of a person, has lead to countless stories of changed lives. I heard a speaker talk about an experiment that was conducted at UC Berkley some years ago, looking at the physiology of overcoming depression versus the chemical manipulation of overcoming depression. The researchers wanted to see if psychotropic drugs or physiology had a more positive impact on a person. They divided the subjects into three groups, as they normally do, and the research began. The first group was given anti-depressants in a normal dosage. They were expected to take the drugs for approximately 15 months. The second group of participants were given a placebo, a fake pill, but told that it was real. The third group was required to smile in front of a mirror for 20 minutes per day. They weren't given any drugs, just "smile therapy." The results were amazing!

The people who smiled in the mirror for 20 minutes per day and made themselves look happy overcoming their depression at a startling rate. 98% of them were no longer depressed after only 30 days. Those on the drugs actually did the worst. The placebo group recovered better, by a margin of about 5%. Yet, in both of the groups that were taking pills, about half of the people were no better at the end of the trial than they were at the beginning. To me, this is incredible! Even if your focus area is not on improving your income, improving your life is a great way to go. If you decide to take my happiness challenge as a part of making time for what matters most, you will see things in this world that you may not have realized existed. The challenge is as follows…

1. Smile for 2 minutes in the morning while looking at yourself in the mirror.

2. Read your one word focus areas out loud three times per day.
3. Think only positive thoughts and say only positive things for 7 continuous days. If you slip up, just start again.

It took me an entire year to have seven continuous days of positive thoughts and words. And, it was an incredible year! Today, I work hard to keep my focus on what matters most. I "Just Make Time" for the things that bring me my definition of success in life. And, I remember the one thing that matters most.

Just Make Time
for your priorities!

ABOUT THE AUTHOR

Jody Holland has written 10 books on various topics, ranging from the self-help genre to business to how-to. He is a graduate of Angelo State University and the school of life. Jody has developed more than 3 dozen training programs to help executives achieve at a higher level. He lives in Amarillo, TX with his wife and two kids, where he focuses on succeeding with balance.

Other Books:

Book	Subject	Price	Available
Leadership Evo	Leadership Growth	19.99	Amazon.com
The Quest	Purpose In Life	14.99	Amazon.com
Living The Quest	Living Your Purpose	14.99	Amazon.com
Breakthrough Leadership	Leadership and Overcoming Challenges	19.99	Amazon.com
25 Activities In A Bag	Portable Team Building Activities	9.99	Amazon.com
Turn Me On	Giving Great Presentations	14.99	Amazon.com

Made in the USA
Columbia, SC
23 December 2019

85598933R00043